Taking Seizure Disorders to School

A Story About Epilepsy

Taking Seizure Disorders To School
Copyright © 1996, by Kim Gosselin.
First Edition. All rights reserved. No part of this book may be reproduced in any manner whatsoever without written permission from the publisher. For information address JayJo Books, LLC, P.O. Box 213, Valley Park, MO 63088-0213. Printed in the United States of America.

Published by
JayJo Books, LLC
P.O. Box 213
Valley Park, MO 63088-0213

Edited by Barbara A. Mitchell

Library of Congress Cataloging-in-Publication Data
Gosselin, Kim
Taking Seizure Disorders to School/Kim Gosselin – First Edition
Library of Congress Catalog Card Number 95-81787
1. Juvenile/Non-Fiction/Health Related
2. Education
3. Medical

ISBN 0-9639449-3-2
Library of Congress

Third Book in our *"Special Kids in School"* series.

Acknowledgements

My heartfelt thanks to all the very giving physicians, educators, and those at the Epilepsy Foundation, St. Louis, Missouri, for their time and support. And truly, a very special "thank you" to the real "Jamie" and her generous mother for allowing me into their lives. Without all of you, this book may never have been written.

*The opinions expressed in **Taking Seizure Disorders to School** are those solely of the author as derived from conducting various interviews and personal research. Seizure disorder care is highly individualized. One should **never** alter seizure disorder care without first consulting a member of the individual's professional seizure disorder or epilepsy medical team.

A portion of the sale of this book is donated specifically to help fund medical research and education. Thank you for your support.

All books published by JayJo Books, LLC are available at special quantity discounts when purchased in bulk by corporations, organizations, or groups. Special imprints, messages and excerpts can be produced to meet your needs. For more information, call 800-801-0159.

A Note from the Author

As the mother of two children living with special health concerns (insulin dependent diabetes and asthma), I soon became aware of a tremendous void in our educational system. Although I found plenty of information for me (and some for teachers), none addressed my children's conditions as they pertained to their peers in the classroom. For my kids, this was a number one priority!

No child likes to be singled out as being "different," much less tormented or teased because of a medical condition. I firmly believe that ignorance is not bliss! All children deserve to be educated regarding the special needs of their classmates.

Taking Seizure Disorders to School was designed and written to be read aloud in the child's classroom. If you don't feel comfortable reading aloud ask the teacher, school nurse, counselor, or perhaps even the children themselves. Try to make it a fun and special event by getting them involved, especially during the short "quiz" found at the end of this book.

Perhaps, someday, the world and those within it will shed a little more understanding and acceptance on those not so fortunate. That is the goal to which I strive, for my children, and for yours.

Kim Gosselin

*This book is dedicated to all children
living with seizure disorders.
And of course, to Wendi and Jaime,
with love and understanding.*

Hello boys and girls! My name is Jaime, and I'm a kid living with a seizure disorder. Epilepsy is another name for seizure disorders. Having epilepsy means part of my brain doesn't always work exactly the way it is supposed to. Because of this, sometimes I may look or act differently than I normally do.

Everybody has a brain, but not everybody has epilepsy.

Have you ever turned on the television after walking across the carpeting in your stocking feet? Did you feel something tingly, or see a little spark? This is kind of what happens inside my brain that makes me have a seizure.

Little "sparks" make my brain send "mixed-up" messages to other parts of my body. Then I begin to have a seizure.

Doctors and nurses don't know why I have epilepsy. I didn't do anything wrong, and it's **nobody's** fault! It's okay to play with me and be my friend.

I can't give you epilepsy or make you have a seizure.

There are many different kinds of seizures. Kids with epilepsy can have one or more kinds of seizures (like me). They can happen any time of the day or night. Medicine helps control my seizures, but it doesn't stop me from having them altogether. Sometimes though, my body gives me a "signal" that a seizure might be coming. This is called an "aura."

An "aura" really is just like a tiny, tiny seizure. It sometimes comes before a bigger seizure. It can make me want to go to a safe place.

When I have a seizure, you might see me sitting at my desk acting like I'm not paying attention. I might stare off into "space" or look like I'm dreaming about something. My eyes might blink a lot, or start to roll. This kind of seizure usually only lasts a few seconds, but it can happen many, many times during the day.

I can't stop myself from having a seizure. After a seizure is over, I may have a headache, or need to take a little rest in the nurse's office.

One kind of seizure can look a little scary to someone who's never seen it before. This seizure usually makes me go unconscious (like a sudden sleep). Sometimes I make strange-sounding noises, or do other things I normally wouldn't do. My body gets very stiff and then starts to shake. Please don't be afraid of me. You might even help me by telling the teacher or school nurse.

The teacher can help too, by turning me on my side and staying with me until the seizure is over. Don't ever try to stop my seizure, and never put anything in my mouth. And NO, it's **not** true that I could swallow my tongue during a seizure. It's not even possible!

Remember, a seizure is just something my body needs to do. It's really nothing to be afraid of.

1. DO NOT PANIC!

2. REMEMBER: A SEIZURE MIGHT LOOK SCARY, BUT IT'S SOMETHING MY BODY NEEDS TO DO.

3. A SEIZURE SHOULD ONLY LAST A FEW MINUTES.

When I first found out I had epilepsy, doctors and nurses worked very hard to find out what kind of seizures I had. This helped them decide what kind of medicine was best for me, and how much to give me. I still go for "check-ups" where they measure how much medicine is in my blood. This helps keep my seizures in good control.

I take my medicine at home and also at school. It's important to take it whenever the doctors and nurses have told me to, and always on time!

Has anyone noticed the special bracelet I always wear? On the back it tells that I have epilepsy. It also has a phone number to call in case of emergency (like if I had a seizure that lasted longer than a few minutes, or if I got in an accident). The people who answer the phone can tell the caller about epilepsy and how to take special care of me.

I never take my bracelet off. It's very important to me and can even help keep me safe!

Because I may have seizures during the school day, sometimes I need a little more time to finish my work. I'd like my teachers and classmates to understand that I'm not goofing off or being lazy when I'm having a seizure!

Kids with seizure disorders aren't dumb or stupid! Sometimes we just need a little extra time to "catch up."

Having seizures is only a very small part of who I am. During most of the school day I'm doing all the same things that you are. I like to play at recess, go to art and gym class, and have lots of friends too!

Having epilepsy doesn't stop me from doing anything other kids do! Sometimes I just need to be a little extra careful.

Maybe someday there will be a cure for seizure disorders. That means my doctors and nurses will be able to fix them! Until then, please don't be afraid of me, or treat me any differently just because I have epilepsy.

After all, nobody's perfect. In fact, I bet I'm a lot like you in every other way!

The End

Let's Take The Seizure Disorder Kids Quiz!

1. What part of my body causes me to have seizures?
My brain.

2. Can you catch a seizure disorder from me, or anybody else?
No, seizure disorders are not contagious!

3. Did I do anything wrong to cause my seizure disorder?
No, and it's nobody's fault, either!

4. How long do most seizures last?
Usually only a few seconds or minutes, at the most.

5. If you see me have a seizure at school, what can you do to help me?
a. Tell the teacher or school nurse.
b. Help me to my side.
c. Stay with me.
d. All of the above.

d. All of the above.

6. Should you put anything in my mouth when I'm having a seizure?
Absolutely not!

Now turn the page to finish the quiz. →

7. Is it possible for me to swallow my tongue during a seizure?
No, it's not even possible.

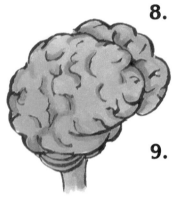

8. Name five things that may tell you I'm having a seizure.
1. Staring off into space 2. Rolling my eyes 3. Falling to the ground 4. Making strange noises 5. Stiff and shaking body.

9. What is the "signal" called that sometimes tells me I'm going to have a seizure?
An "aura".

10. Can I stop myself from having seizures?
No, medicine helps control them, but it doesn't stop them from happening altogether.

11. Does having a seizure disorder stop me from doing anything other kids do?
Not usually. Sometimes I just need to be a little extra careful.

12. Should you treat me any differently just because I have a seizure disorder?
No. Just be patient and understanding. Remember, I'm a lot like you in every other way!

Great job! Thanks for taking the Seizure Disorder Kids Quiz and learning more about epilepsy!

To order additional copies of **Taking Seizure Disorders to School** contact your local bookstore or library. Or call the publisher directly at (314) 861-1331 or (800) 801-0159. Write to us at:

JayJo Books, LLC
P.O. Box 213
Valley Park, MO 63088-0213

Ask about our special quantity discounts for schools, hospitals, and affiliated organizations.

Look for other books by Kim Gosselin including

Taking Diabetes to School

Taking Asthma to School

Taking Asthma to Camp
(A Fictional Story About Asthma Camp)

. . . and new titles coming soon including **"Zooallergy!"**

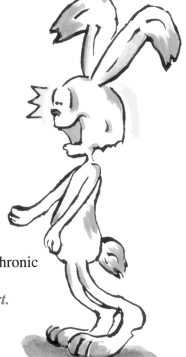

A portion of the proceeds from all our publications are donated to various charities to help fund important medical research and education.

We work hard to make a difference in the lives of children with chronic conditions and/or special needs.

Thank you for your support.

Ask about future books in our *"Special Kids in School"* series!